AN EXPLANATION OF POETRY
TO MY FATHER

An Explanation of Poetry to My Father

Glenn Colquhoun

illustrations by Nikki Slade Robinson

STEELE ROBERTS LTD
AOTEAROA NEW ZEALAND

To my Mum
And to my Dad
Who made me good
And made me bad.

Second printing 2003
Third printing 2008

978-1-877228-44-5

STEELE ROBERTS LTD
BOX 9321, WELLINGTON
info@steeleroberts.co.nz • www.SteeleRoberts.co.nz

with the support of

ARTS COUNCIL OF NEW ZEALAND *TOI AOTEAROA*

Contents

An apology

I was not a son to take the Word
of God to the whole world.

I was not a son to spot a fine
cow at auction.

I was not a son who was able to
fix the inside of dark engines.

I did not win the game
in its final minute.

I was not a son to sweat all day
on the end of a shovel.

I was not a son to remain calm
at the sight of my own blood.

I was not a son to capture the
hearts of beautiful women.

I did not save for a rainy day.

I was not a son to discover
the cures to rare illnesses.

I was not a son to bear you
a generation of fine children.

I was a son who believed
in the making of poetry.

Which is, I suppose, in the end,
pretty much the same thing.

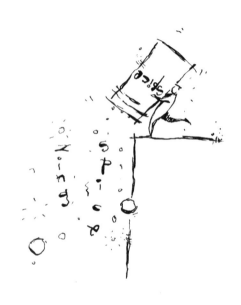

The first lesson

Now are you going to listen or not? There's nothing tricky about a poem. It's just a collection of words like one of those bunches of grapes that used to hang in the backyard, how every one had a particular shape depending on the way it grew, or like one of those macramé pot-holders Aunty Jean used to make except the words are the knots and at each one you can change direction, or like when Mum cooks and some words are like mince and cheap and easy to fill you up with and contain most of what's good for you and those are the ones she uses a lot and some words are spicy so she only uses them a little bit and like some words look so good she uses them for colour and others act differently under heat, cheese for example, to melt all through a poem which is great unless you don't like cheese. Some bits might stick in your teeth for days unless you brush them and I know you don't always do that. Maybe if you think of words like cars on a motorway, how if they are speeding or not being driven carefully they can easily lose control and cause an accident and then another car will hit them and then a truck and before you know it there is a huge pile-up with everyone tut-tutting, well the pile-up can be a poem too. Sometimes you'll even find poems like Grandad did with that piece of driftwood which looked like a woman with her legs crossed and if you're lucky no-one else has pinched it so you can pick it up off the ground and put your name on it and the ladies at church will wonder why on earth you have that in the garden. It can even be like when you're laying cobblestones and every word fits neatly into the next so that sometimes there's a pattern if you stand back far enough, or if you're laying bricks, how you have to knock words in half to fit them into the end of sentences so the next layer has something to build onto and all you do all day is look at bricks and when you put your head up there's a whole wall or a house with windows and corners that you're surprised is there and while we're talking about bricks sometimes you can put words together because of the way they look, brown bricks or red bricks or rough bricks or smooth bricks so people can enjoy them like when we go for a drive through Howick and Mum likes the colour of the houses, and sometimes you can put them together because they hold things up and are strong and have a use even if no-one sees them, bricks don't really have a sound unless you drop them on your foot and then they make a sound that sounds like bloody hell, and sometimes when you read a poem you feel like it doesn't even belong on the paper or that you've seen it before somewhere or should have seen it before or always meant to make one just like it and so if you turn around it will move behind your back, sometimes it's like a child who makes you drop him off up the road from school so his mates won't see you kiss him goodbye and then shoos you away as if to say 'don't make such a fuss' but the way I like to think of poems the most is that they are like a lolly for your mind or an argument with a clever person who is always trying to put words into your mouth and then spends the rest of the day trying to take them back out again.

The Page Three Girl

1. In the beginning was the word. And the word was with God. And the word was God. Then the word became flesh and dwelt among us.

2. At first the word was a German housewife. Simon the mechanic said she reminded him of *A History of the World in Eight Volumes.* He left her sitting on the shelf.

3. Next the word was a nun. Barry the gib-stopper was as interested in her as he was in reading the Bible.

4. Then the word became a solo mother with three kids who had just been left by a troubled husband found spying on his boss for a foreign government until he ran away with her. Dave the cabinet-maker said she was as complicated as a novel.

5. Next the word was an actress. Dick the electrician fell asleep when he found out there were no car chases in her script.

6. Later the word was a barmaid. Vic the bricklayer quickly made off with her as though she was a Sunday newspaper tucked firmly underneath his arm.

7. At last the word appeared as naked as a poem. Mum found her hiding underneath my mattress. I said heavens. She said hell. You said Jesus, Mary and Joseph. And all Jeff the plumber ever said was God!

The shape of words

A is the shape of a tin roof on an old church.

B is the bottom of a fat man.

C is a crab scuttling along the beach.

X is the shape of butterfly wings.

hallelujah is the shape of righteous people sitting closely together in church.

abracadabra is a caterpillar crawling along its leaf.

bubbling is the shape of water boiling.

higgledypiggledy is a collection of flowers dripping out of their window boxes.

daddy-long-legs are small carts unloading suitcases from the back of an aeroplane.

orange is the shape of a round fruit hanging from a tree, a young woman reaching out to pick it, a kitten chasing after its own tail, an old woman weeding her garden, a small boy fishing from a pond, the sun setting over a smooth beach.

smoke is a lazy snake crawling towards the sun, two large clouds billowing, a round mouth coughing, a small bird singing in a tree, the eye of a tired child falling asleep.

love is one leg planted firmly on the ground, a spare washer for a dripping tap, that beautiful bird flying towards me or away, a broken eggshell opened on the floor.

The sound of words

A-B-C-D-E-F-G-H-I-J-K-L-M-N-O-P
Rain falling on a tin roof.

One-Two-Three-Four-Five-Six-Seven-Eight
The feet of marching girls as precise as tape.

She Sells Sea Shells by the Sea Shore
Cars passing cautiously along wet roads at night.

Ka mate Ka mate Ka ora Ka ora
Morepork calling inside a dark forest.

Old MacDonald had a farm E-I-E-I-O
A round ball rolling off the end of the front porch.

Bee-bop-a-loo-baa-a-wop-bam-boom
A can of paint falling down a ladder.

Romeo Romeo Wherefore art thou Romeo
A man revving his motorcycle outside
a woman's house.

Etcetera-Etcetera-Etcetera-Etcetera
Crickets warming themselves underneath
a drying sun.

**Ourfatherwhoartinheavenhallowedbethy
namethykingdomcomethywillbedoneon
earthasitisinheaven**
A bee trapped uncomfortably inside
a closed room.

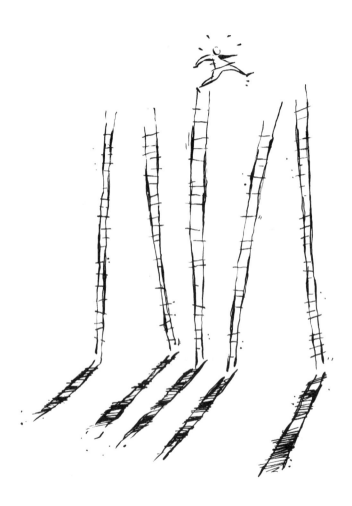

The meaning of words

1. Either

```
T T S A L I T P T I P N
H H H N I T O A H N R O
E E O D K W F U E G E T
C R U D E O O S S O C H
H I L O U R E P F A   I
I G D W A L G F E B R N
N H B N D D E O C A I G
E T E I D B T R L O B
S I W N E E W A A U U
E D R A R D H B C N S
H E I R S I E R U C L
A A T O T F N E L I Y
V W T W H F W A A N O
E O E E I E T R G V
  R N   N C H F   E A
  D U     C   F   R I
  S P     U   E   R
          L   E
          T   L
```

2. Or

Words are halfbacks.

They don't scrum.

They don't ruck.

They don't maul.

They don't jump.

They don't throw into lineouts.

They don't carry oranges at half-time.

They don't argue with the referee.

They just pass —

Ideas as quick as bullets.

God help you

if you drop them!

Poetry is a game

But so is footy

And we all know how serious that is.

The word as a wrapping

It would help if you think of words
as wrappings

That plain brown paper a butcher uses
to surround steak

The newsprint announcing your fish and chips

A patterned cloth spread over the kitchen table
like butter on a slice of bread

All circles: such as the letter O, open mouths,
diamond rings, key-rings, keyholes, portholes,
plugholes, life-savers, lipstick stains, washers for
taps, the rim of soap left around a bath when
the water is let out

All containers: such as cups and saucers, salad
bowls, hot-water bottles, pot-plant holders,
schoolbags, jam-jars, fruit tins, ashtrays, woven
baskets, plastic milk bottles and hollows in the
stumps of trees

All pipes: such as drainpipes, downpipes, sewer pipes, exhaust pipes, spouting, U-bends, gutters, stormwater drains, inner tubes, brandy snaps and hydroslides

Eggshells
        Seashells
      Cigarette papers
             Soap holders
     Cellophane
                 Raincoats
       Fur coats
                Wrap-around skirts
  Hot air balloons
       Soap bubbles

Sunglasses worn by a particular friend you cannot recognise without them

Brightly patterned lolly papers picked up by the wind and bounced against the concrete-coloured pavement of the sky.

clinging defiantly to ledge

The word as a means of communication

Above everything else
the word is an attempt
to end isolation

Fingertips of heroes
clinging defiantly
to ledges

Small boats
sailed fearlessly
on wide oceans

That grass
which grows from
the armpits of concrete

Those temporary footsteps
at regular intervals
of Captain Scott
disappearing in the snow.

The word as a memory

Not everyone agrees that blue
is the correct word for a fine sky.

For parents of children who have drowned
in deep water blue is the colour of dying.

For lovers undressed silently by the light
of the moon blue is the colour of desire.

For travellers who wander the edges of
mountains blue is the colour of horizons.

For the lonely left aching by scandalous
lovers blue is the colour of music.

For soldiers who have died in defence
of their flag blue is the colour of glory.

For children raised on a street of brick houses
blue is the colour of rebellion.

For thieves who have been asked to empty
their pockets blue is the colour of policemen.

For women who love men with indigo eyes
blue is the colour of swimming.

For undertakers who apply lipstick to the
mouths of the dead blue is the colour of ice.

For dogs who have been fed from blue plastic
bowls blue is the colour of a full stomach.

The word as a tool

Language is as full of tools as the inside of a hardware store.

Nouns are everything you can make something out of, four-by-twos, six-by-twos, three-by-one-and-a-halves, weatherboards, ceiling battens, PVC, gib-board, aluminium windows, bricks, doors, tiles, carpet, concrete reinforcing rods and all types of spouting.

Articles are builders' pencils, used for making marks, drawing arrows, stirring tea or placing behind an ear when you're working.

It is no coincidence that **commas** come in the shape of chisels perfect for breaking up that overlong sentence with too many words which no-one can stop because one thought leads into another and then into another again until you have forgotten how it all started anyway and now it won't fit into the back of the ute.

Verbs are Estwing hammers, 20 ounce, full metal shaft, comfortable plastic composite handles with a non-slip grip and claw head. Ideal for putting some whack into a sentence. They come in black and blue and have a good feel hung from a leather pouch firm against your thigh.

Rhyme is the ratchet on a socket, two steps forward and one step back. Use it to draw words as tight as wire against their fenceposts.

Ellipses are screwdriver sets — Philips, slotheads, Allen keys in a full range of sizes. They can be used to increase the torque inside a poem.

Rhythm is a tape measure, one of those ones that rolls up into a case, or a ruler that folds out and then folds out again so you can lay it down beside a sentence and mark off the metres.

Conjunctions are all screws (roundheads, countersunk, self-tappers), nails (flatheads, jolts, galvanised and bright), clouts, staples, PVA glue or polyfilla and whatever else you use to cover up the gaps between words.

Alliteration / Consonance / Assonance are grades of sandpaper — for obtaining that extra smooth finish. The trick is to make everyone think you haven't used them.

Similes and Metaphors are rolled up sets of plans carried underneath your armpit or in the back seat of the truck that someone else has spilt their coffee on. A place where what you are putting together has already been put together, or if that doesn't make sense, it's what you meant when you always said after taking the nail off your thumb with a blunt hammer that the mongrel bled like a stuck pig.

Tyger Tyger burning bright in the forests of the night what immortal hand or eye could frame thy fearful symmetry — the word as a member of the local community

Poems are small villages occupied by words.

Tyger is, by the sound of it, a local cat.

Immortal a priest dying of cirrhosis.

Fearful is a housewife whose husband ignores her. She never likes to leave the house.

Symmetry is her partner. His body is sculptured from working out at the gym. He is notoriously unfaithful.

Of and **Or** are sisters. One forms dependent relationships. The other can never seem to make up her mind.

What is a schoolteacher
who always has an answer to everything.

Hand props up the local bar.

In is the publican. She is buxom and blonde.

Mr **Burning** is a fireman, a hero during the war.
He drives an ice-cream van on weekends.

Bright is his deputy who is dull.

The is the milkman who always seems
to show up everywhere.

Thy is his father who is retired
but still does the odd delivery.

Frame is a builder. He has played prop
for the local rugby team ever since he was a boy.

Forests is the gardener who knows
the names of trees.

Night is a burglar. He lives in an old house
at the far end of town.

Miss **Could** is a spinster who wonders what might have happened if she had run away with the butcher's son when she was a girl.

Eye is their policeman watching through his window, round as the moon in the middle of the night

rearranging pencils against the top of his desk

making sure everyone around him
is serving their sentence.

Balance the
poem in
the palm
of your hand

A set of instructions to be used when reading a poem

1. To begin with lift the poem carefully out of its paper.

2. Balance the poem in the palm of your hand.

3. Don't be afraid of the poem.

4. Run your fingers around the outside of the poem:

   a. Is it rough or smooth?
   b. Is it heavy or light?

5. Throw the poem up into the air. Does it float?

6. Put the poem into your mouth. Either:

   a. Squeeze a small amount onto
      your tongue like toothpaste

   b. Enter the whole poem
      into your mouth like cake

7. Remove the first word and the last word from the poem. Shake vigorously. Each word should fall out of line.

8. Place the words into your mouth and roll them around. Suck. Chew. Gargle. Hide the words in your cheeks. Spit them at people.

9. When you are finished put the words back where they belong.

10. Whisper the poem quietly to yourself.

11. Yell the poem out loud.

12. Recite the poem in broad daylight / in moonlight / with the lights on / with the lights off / in the bathroom / in the garden / underneath a tree.

13. Recite the poem on fine days / on rainy days / on calm days / on windy days / on an empty stomach / with your mouth full.

14. Put the poem on blocks and lie underneath it. Tinker with the timing. Pack each word in grease. File off the engine numbers. Repaint the poem.

15. Eat breakfast on the poem. Stain the poem with coffee.

16. Stand on the poem.

17. Water the poem.

18. Mix the poem in with the washing.

19. Carry the poem around in your pocket for a week.

20. Now the poem belongs to you.

To a man of few words

Old King, in the end
what I mean to say
is that a poem is just like you.

These obvious criteria:

    two arms, two legs
    a head, one belly
    warm blood, tough sinew
    wet tears, snot
    muscle and eyes.

Those hidden lines:

    unsaid, undone
    unfinished, unwound
    uncomfortable
    unexplained
    unspoken.

All that is not said

The riddle of you

That gap between us.

A place I sometimes come to
at the edge of my skin

like the lookout up on One Tree Hill
to stare across at Rangitoto

wondering how you can be both out
there and inside of me at the same time.

In other words

A poem is a way
of knowing you are alive

As shocking as fish
leaping out of deep water

As sharp as light stabbing
through a row of trees

As bold as opening up
your eyes during prayer

As simple as lying awake
in the middle of the night
listening to the sound
of people snoring

Every minute
of every day
of every life

is a full library

The last word

One day I saw
a bird flying

Without strings

Without wire

Without obvious attachment.

There were no instruments
to measure altitude

No fine pencil-marks made
by engineers when constructing
the elegance of machinery.

It was as though the sky
was not blue and empty
but filled by patterns

One of which was
cleaved like strong wind
by soft paper.

All I have wanted
is to ache for words
as clean as that.

Also by Glenn Colquhoun

The Art of Walking Upright
Winner of the best first book award for poetry,
Montana New Zealand Book Awards, 2000.

Playing God
Winner of the poetry and the readers' choice awards,
Montana New Zealand Book Awards 2003.

Mr Short, Mr Thin, Mr Bald & Mr Dog
A wacky children's picture book, illustrated by
Nikki Slade Robinson.

How We Fell
This innovative collection about a ten-year
relationship is for anyone who has ever fallen
in – or out – of love.

PUBLISHED BY STEELE ROBERTS